ISBN: 9798329916669

Website: www.jdalearning.com

Email: jdalearning@gmail.com

Youtube Educational Videos: www.youtube.com/c/JadyAlvarez

Instagram: www.instagram.com/jadyahomeschool

Alphabet Manuscript

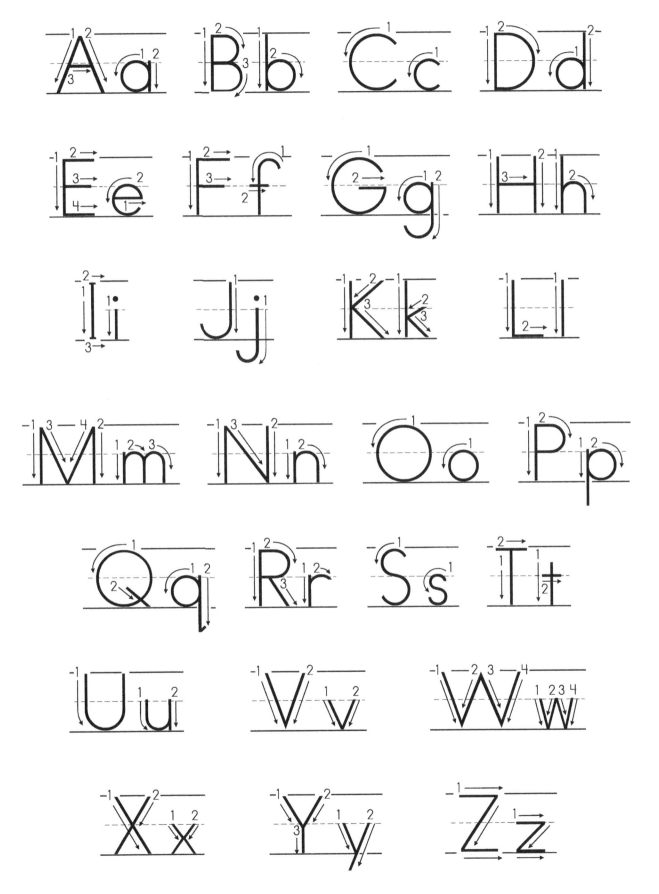

Read the word, write the word, and circle the consonant letter blend. A consonant letter blend contains two consonants.

bl

blab

blab

bled

blip

blob

blog

Read the word, write the word, and circle the consonant letter blend.

br

brag

bran

brat

bred

brim

Read the word, write the word, and circle the consonant letter blend.

th

than

that

them

then

this

Read the word, write the word, and circle the consonant letter blend.

ch

chap

_____

chat

_____

chin

_____

chop

_____

chug

_____

Read the word, write the word, and circle the consonant letter blend.

cl

clam

clap

clip

clot

club

Read the word, write the word, and circle the consonant letter blend.

cr

crab

crest

crib

crop

crust

Read the word, write the word, and circle the consonant letter blend.

dr

drab

_____

drag

_____

drip

_____

drop

_____

drum

_____

Read the word, write the word, and circle the consonant letter blend.

fl

flag

flat

fled

flip

flop

Read the word, write the word, and circle the consonant letter blend.

fr

frag

frat

Fred

fret

frog

Read the word, write the word, and circle the consonant letter blend.

gl

glad

glam

glib

glob

glut

Read the word, write the word, and circle the consonant letter blend.

gr

grab _____

gram _____

grid _____

grin _____

grip _____

Read the word, write the word, and circle the consonant letter blend.

pl

plan

pleb

plot

plug

plum

Read the word, write the word, and circle the consonant letter blend.

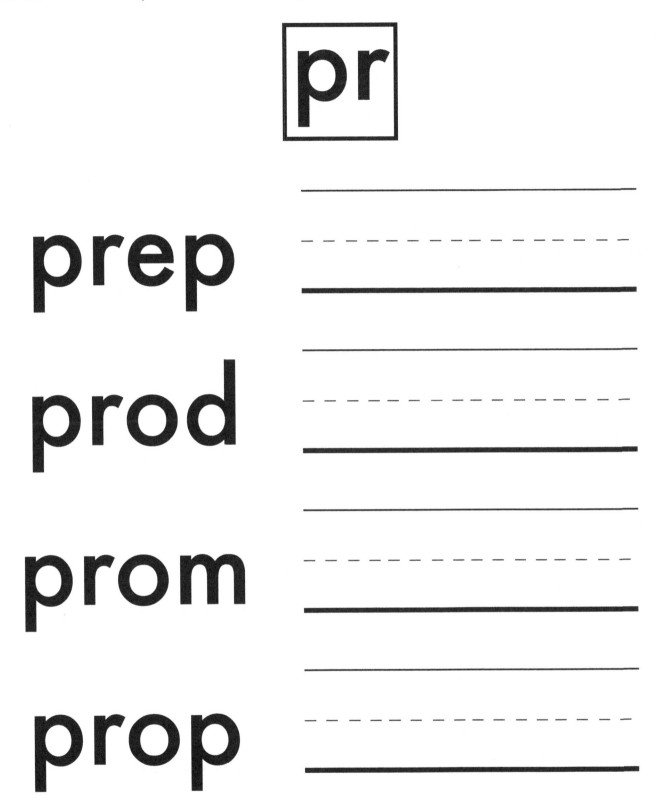

pr

prep

prod

prom

prop

Read the word, write the word, and circle the consonant letter blend.

sc

scab

_____

scam

_____

scan

_____

scud

_____

scum

_____

Read the word, write the word, and circle the consonant letter blend.

sl

slap

_____
- - - - - - - -
_____

sled

_____
- - - - - - - -
_____

slim

_____
- - - - - - - -
_____

slot

_____
- - - - - - - -
_____

slug

_____
- - - - - - - -
_____

Read the word, write the word, and circle the consonant letter blend.

sm

smack

_____

smash

_____

smell

_____

smog

_____

smug

_____

Read the word, write the word, and circle the consonant letter blend.

sn

snag

_____

snap

_____

snip

_____

snot

_____

snug

_____

Read the word, write the word, and circle the consonant letter blend.

sp

span

sped

spin

spot

spun

Read the word, write the word, and circle the consonant letter blend.

st

stem

_____

step

_____

stop

_____

stud

_____

stun

_____

Read the word, write the word, and circle the consonant letter blend.

sw

swam

_____

swim

_____

swell

_____

swept

_____

swift

_____

Read the word, write the word, and circle the consonant letter blend.

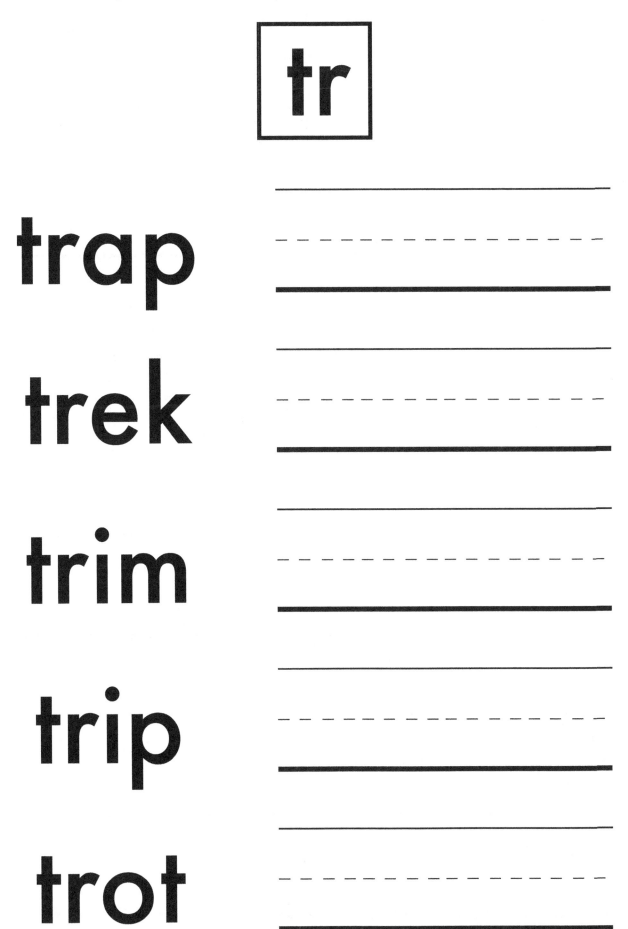

tr

trap

trek

trim

trip

trot

Write the words in the correct order to make a sentence.
A sentence _always begins with a capital letter_ and _always ends with a period (punctuation)._

	bug the red is

	sun hot is the

	pet I a have

Write the words in the correct order to make a sentence. A sentence _always begins with a capital letter_ and _always ends with a period (punctuation)_.

hen   the   ran

sat   fox   the

Jeff   net   has   a

Write the words in the correct order to make a sentence. A sentence _always begins with a capital letter_ and _always ends with a period (punctuation)_.

bell   the   rang

_ _

_ _

ran   dog   the

_ _

_ _

pink   is   pig   the

_ _

_ _

Write the words in the correct order to make a sentence. A sentence _always begins with a capital letter_ and _always ends with a period (punctuation)_.

can hop Tom

is black hat the

crab red the is

Write the words in the correct order to make a sentence. A sentence _always begins with a capital letter_ and _always ends with a period (punctuation)_.

blast   a   had   Jim

_____

_____

is   cat   mad   the

_____

_____

fast   Brad   ran

_____

_____

Write the words in the correct order to make a sentence. A sentence _always begins with a capital letter_ and _always ends with a period (punctuation)_.

sad	hog	this	is

_____

_____

Ken	the	cup	drops

_____

_____

flip	a	did	Sam

_____

_____

Write the words in the correct order to make a sentence. A sentence _always begins with a capital letter_ and _always ends with a period (punctuation)._

flag   Pat   a   has

bat   a   got   Jim

the   I   cut   tag

Write the words in the correct order to make a sentence.
A sentence _always begins with a capital letter_ and _always ends with a period (punctuation)._

hop   did   frog   the

has   plan   a   Dad

ant   the   red   is

Write the words in the correct order to make a sentence. A sentence _always begins with a capital letter_ and _always ends with a period (punctuation)_.

bag   mom   a   has

_ _

pot   the   has   lid   a

_ _

Dan   pen   a   has

_ _

Write the words in the correct order to make a sentence. A sentence _always begins with a capital letter_ and _always ends with a period (punctuation)_.

fed   dog   his   Bob

_ _ _ _ _ _ _ _ _ _ _ _ _ _ _ _ _ _

a   Pat   doll   has

_ _ _ _ _ _ _ _ _ _ _ _ _ _ _ _ _ _

in Ted swims the pond

_ _ _ _ _ _ _ _ _ _ _ _ _ _ _ _ _ _

Write the words in the correct order to make a sentence. A sentence <u>always begins with a capital letter</u> and <u>always ends with a period (punctuation)</u>.

will twig the snap

cap Ben the twists

the big is rat

Write the words in the correct order to make a sentence. A sentence _always begins with a capital letter_ and _always ends with a period (punctuation)._

in   bus   is   Ben   the

_ _ _ _ _ _ _ _ _ _ _ _ _ _ _

_ _ _ _ _ _ _ _ _ _ _ _ _ _ _

a   gift   Ron   got

_ _ _ _ _ _ _ _ _ _ _ _ _ _ _

_ _ _ _ _ _ _ _ _ _ _ _ _ _ _

lift   Sam   box   the   can

_ _ _ _ _ _ _ _ _ _ _ _ _ _ _

_ _ _ _ _ _ _ _ _ _ _ _ _ _ _

Write the words in the correct order to make a sentence. A sentence _always begins with a capital letter_ and _always ends with a period (punctuation)._

dress   the   red   is

_ _

_ _

hill   up   ran   Tom   the

_ _

_ _

bed the jumps on dog the

_ _

_ _

Write the words in the correct order to make a sentence. A sentence _always begins with a capital letter_ and _always ends with a period (punctuation)._

hog   is   the   fat

ink   pen   red   the   has

on   bed   his   Dan   slept

Write the words in the correct order to make a sentence. A sentence _always begins with a capital letter_ and _always ends with a period (punctuation)_.

black pot the is hot

_____

_____

Jen big hat has a

_____

_____

is box fox the in the

_____

_____

Copy the sentence and circle all of the consonant letter blends.

Kim went to the bus stop.

Copy the sentence and circle all of the consonant letter blends.

That big

red fox is

mad.

_____

- - - - - - - - - - - - -

_____

_____

- - - - - - - - - - - - -

_____

_____

- - - - - - - - - - - - -

_____

Copy the sentence and circle all of the consonant letter blends.

Pam swam

in the

pond.

Copy the sentence and circle all of the consonant letter blends.

Tom claps

and Pam

sings.

Copy the sentence and circle all of the consonant letter blends.

The bell in
the church
rang.

Copy the sentence and circle all of the consonant letter blends.

Jan's red
doll is soft.

Copy the sentence and circle all of the consonant letter blends.

Dan went fast on the sled.

Copy the sentence and circle all of the consonant letter blends.

The stem of the plant is long.

Copy the sentence and circle all of the consonant letter blends.

Ben and

Ken are

twins.

Copy the sentence and circle all of the consonant letter blends.

The ship
had a
wreck.

Copy the sentence and circle all of the consonant letter blends.

Mom hurt
her wrist in
the park.

Copy the sentence and circle all of the consonant letter blends.

The hen
pecks at
the tick.

_____

- - - - - - - - - - - - - - - - - - -

_____

_____

- - - - - - - - - - - - - - - - - - -

_____

- - - - - - - - - - - - - - - - - - -

_____

Copy the sentence and circle all of the consonant letter blends.

The rock in
the pond is
black.

_____

- - - - - - - - - - - - - - - - -

_____

_____

- - - - - - - - - - - - - - - - -

_____

_____

- - - - - - - - - - - - - - - - -

_____

Copy the sentence and circle all of the consonant letter blends.

The frog
sits on the
log.

Copy the sentence and circle all of the consonant letter blends.

Jill got red socks as a gift.

Dictation Sentences

Read these sentences to the student and have them write one sentence a day. Have the child use phonics to sound out the words and write them as best as they can. When they are done have the child draw a picture.

1) The hen sat in the pen.
2) The brim of the hat is red.
3) Chad went up the hill.
4) Sam has a black bat.
5) Mom has a hot pot.
6) Pam has a big drum set.
7) The frog sat on the log.
8) The red fox ran into a den.
9) Jim is in the red van.
10) Ann went to the park.
11) Dad will prep the lunch bag.
12) Jill fell and got hurt.
13) Tom went fast on his sled.
14) The pig was big and pink.
15) Ken has a dog with black spots.

© 2024 JDA Learning Resources LLC

Listen to the sentence, write it, and draw a picture.

1

Listen to the sentence, write it, and draw a picture.

2

Listen to the sentence, write it, and draw a picture.

3

Listen to the sentence, write it, and draw a picture.

4

Listen to the sentence, write it, and draw a picture.

5

Listen to the sentence, write it, and draw a picture.

6

Listen to the sentence, write it, and draw a picture.

7

Listen to the sentence, write it, and draw a picture.

8

Listen to the sentence, write it, and draw a picture.

9

Listen to the sentence, write it, and draw a picture.

10

Listen to the sentence, write it, and draw a picture.

11

Listen to the sentence, write it, and draw a picture.

12

Listen to the sentence, write it, and draw a picture.

13

Listen to the sentence, write it, and draw a picture.

14

Listen to the sentence, write it, and draw a picture.

15

Write a sentence about the picture.

- -

_____

_____

- -

_____

_____

- -

_____

_____

- -

_____

Write a sentence about the picture.

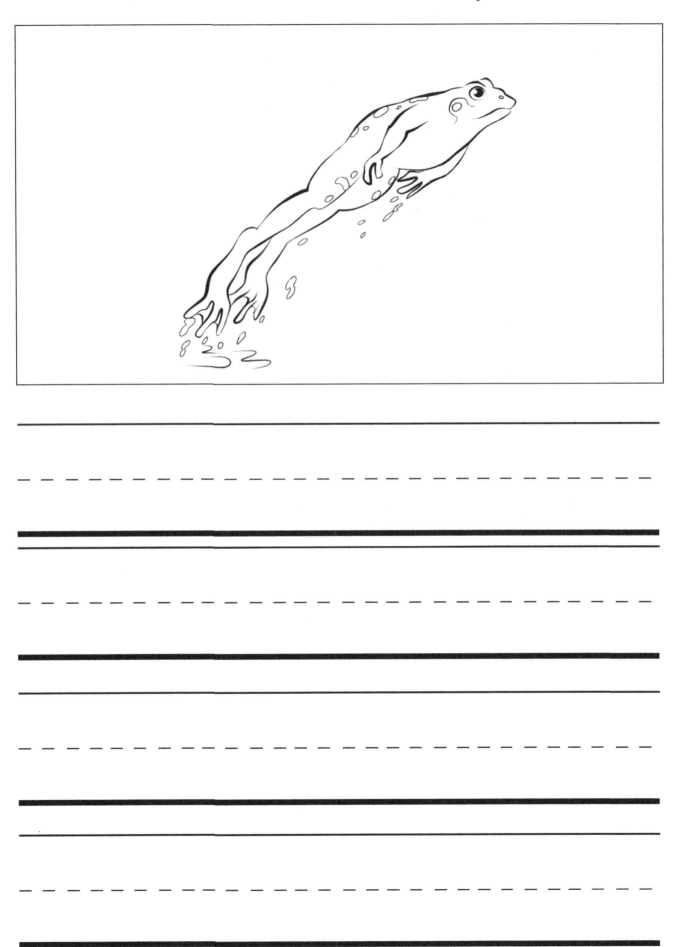

Write a sentence about the picture.

Write a sentence about the picture.

Write a sentence about the picture.

Write a sentence about the picture.

Write a sentence about the picture.

Write a sentence about the picture.

Write a sentence about the picture.

Write a sentence about the picture.

Made in the USA
Columbia, SC
22 October 2024